She

The Unsaid Voice

Pooja Rathod

BookLeaf Publishing

India | USA | UK

Made with ❤ on the BookLeaf Publishing Platform
www.bookleafpub.in
www.bookleafpub.com

Dedication

To my mother,

You are gone,
yet you took a piece of me with you.

I admired you in life,
but only in your absence did I truly understand your
worth.

You live in my heart, my words, and every part of me.
Forever loved, forever missed.

Preface

I never truly understood how the world worked until my mother was gone. Loss has a way of stripping away illusions, revealing truths we once ignored. This book is born from that understanding—from the grief, the heartbreak, and the lessons that only pain can teach. It is a collection of poetry about womanhood, love, loss, and the weight of carrying wounds that are sometimes generations old. It speaks of toxic ties, silent battles, and the resilience that lives within every woman who has ever had to endure. But above all, it is a tribute—to my mother, to the women who came before me, and to those who are still finding their voice. If you have ever loved and lost, if you have ever felt unseen, if you have ever carried the burden of being a woman in a world that does not always make space for you— these words are for you.

Pooja Rathod

Acknowledgements

"I wrote this book for my mother—her love, her absence, and the echoes she left in my soul."

1. WITHOUT YOU

I reach for you, but you're not there,
An empty seat, a whispered prayer.
Yet in my heart, you softly stay,
Guiding me along the way.

2. LOST AT 29

Still stuck at twenty-nine, lost in the haze,
Wandering blindly through endless days.

They ask of my dreams, my purpose, my name,
But I only echo the questions the same.

Who am I, in this maze of doubt?
A whisper unheard, a voice without shout.

They speak of purpose like stars in the sky,
Yet mine fades like embers, too dim to fly.

3. UNSHAKEN

Their scorn may lacerate my soul,
Yet shall not fracture, nor control.

Ephemeral tongues may twist and chide,
But I remain—undaunted, tried.

4. The GIRL WHO WAITS

She walks alone, yet not unkind,
A heart of gold, a thoughtful mind.

At twenty-nine, the world will say,
"Why love has not yet come your way?"

But she just smiles, her soul is free,
No rush, no race, just destiny.

For love, she knows, is not a game,
Nor something built on fleeting fame.

She dreams of hands that hold her tight,
Of whispered words on moonlit nights.

Yet never will she chase or plead,
For love must come, not grow from need.

So let them ask, let voices pry,
She lifts her head, she won't comply.

For when the time is right, she'll see—
Love's not too late, it waits for *thee.*

5. THE NIGHT SHE LEFT

The night she left, the world stood still,
A hollow hush, a bitter chill.

The rain wept hard upon my skin,
As if the sky could feel my sin.

No light within, just endless black,
The past behind, no turning back

.

The dogs, they howled, they sensed her soul,
A ghostly whisper, dark and cold.

I saw her there—a fleeting shade,
A voice that called but never stayed.

I prayed to God, "Take me instead,
Let her return, let me be dead."

But silence fell, no words, no sign,
Just rain and wind, no hand in mine.

And so I stood, alone in pain,
Lost in the night of shadows and rain.

6. HER LAST WORDS TO ME

Though fever burned and breath was weak,
Her voice still soft, so warm, so meek.

Through weary lungs, through aching bone,
She called my name upon the phone.

"Beta, how are you?" she said,
While sickness wrapped around her bed.

Her world was dim, yet she still knew,
No pain could keep her love from view.

Is this the love that knows no end?
That bends but never dares to bend?

A love that fights, a love that stays,
A light that never fades away.

Though time may steal, though fate may call,
A mother's love outlives it all.

7. SHE IS STILL HUMAN

No job, no ring, yet she is whole,
A beating heart, a shining soul.

Not defined by work or place,
She moves through life with strength and grace.

She dreams, she loves, she stands her ground,
Her worth is deep, it knows no bound.

A life is more than titles won—
She is human, like everyone.

8. WHERE WAS GOD

I called His name when mother fell,
But heaven's doors shut tight as well.

No voice, no sign, no saving hand—
Just quiet earth and silent sand.

If God was there, He did not stay,
Or maybe He was far away.

Or maybe, in my mother's eyes,
He lived, then left—when her soul cried.

9. HE LET HER GO

She once believed in whispered prayers,
In love that lived beyond the air.

Her mother told her, soft and bright,
That God would hold them through the night.

But when the light in her mother dimmed,
No angel came, no heavens brimmed.

She cried to God, but none replied,
Just silence where her hope had died.

So now she walks with hollow hands,
No faith, no stars, just sinking sand.

For if He's there, she does not know—
He let her mother go.

10. A HOME WITHOUT WARMTH

She drifts like smoke in a house of stone,
A name they speak in spite, not love.

Her mother's warmth has turned to dust,
And none remain to lift her up.

They carve their words into her skin,
Sharp-edged whispers, hollow grins.

She swallows hurt like bitter rain,
Drowning slow in unseen pain.

No hands to hold, no eyes that see,
Just walls that echo misery.

She wonders if the world would care,
If one day she was never there.

11. THE GIRL WHO STOPPED

She used to find worlds in pages,
Lose herself in stories and dreams.

Now the books sit closed, forgotten,
Like echoes of who she used to be.

She moves because she must,
Breathes because she can.

Nothing matters, nothing stays—
Just hours slipping through her hands.

They call her lazy, call her weak,
As if she chose this hollow ache.

But how do you run when you are sinking?
How do you fight when you are numb?

She stares at screens, at walls, at nothing,
Waiting for a spark, a sign, a reason.

But all she hears is silence.
All she feels is gone.

12. STILL WAITING

13

She gathers their words like broken glass,
Bleeding, but holding on too fast.

Their love is distant, sharp, unkind,
Yet still, she hopes they'll change their mind.

She shrinks herself, she plays their game,
Chasing praise that never came.

She wonders if she'll ever be
Enough for them—enough to see.

13. SHE KNEW, I DIDIN'T

I called her narrow, bound in chains,
A mind too small for my endless dreams.

I thought she feared the open sky,
While I longed to spread my wings and fly.

But now she's gone, and I can see—
She was the wind beneath my feet.

She held the storm, she bore the weight,
She fought for love in silent ways.

My father speaks of rules and walls,
Of what to do, of what must be.

But she, she knew what freedom was—
Not loud rebellion, but quiet release.

She was the choice to stand or kneel,
The voice that soothed, the hands that healed.

And how foolish I had been to miss,
That she was freedom In its purest bliss.

14. THE DAY I DISAPPEARED

They buried her, but not alone,
A part of me sank with the stone.

Now I walk, but not as me,
Just someone else—a memory.

15. INVISIBLE TEARS

I cried in the bathroom, alone in the dark,
Tears falling silent, lost in the spark

Of a phone screen glow—no one could see,
No one was watching, no one but me.

I cried in the kitchen, hands gripping the sink,
Salt in my mouth, too broken to blink.

They walked right past, they laughed, they spoke,
But never once saw that I was choked.

I cried in the night, where shadows keep,
Drenched in sorrow, too tired to sleep.

I cried before them, I cried in crowds,
Yet no one asked, no voice was loud.

Did they not know, or not want to see?
Was I too quiet, or were they just free

Free from the weight, free from the pain,
Free from the loss that drowns me in rain?

16. PRIOSN WITHOU BARS

I want to run, to stand alone,
To build a life that's truly my own.

To earn, to rise, to carve my way,
To break the chains that make me stay.

But freedom feels so far, so weak,
Like a dream too high to ever reach.

Not locked by walls, not tied by hands,
Yet trapped in fears I don't understand.

I whisper *help* but no one hears,
Or maybe they just turn from tears.

So I sit, I wait, I hold my breath—
A caged bird scared to face what's next.

17. BELONGING NOWHERE

I live among them, yet I'm alone,
A ghost in blood, a heart disowned.

Because I am a daughter, unclaimed, unwed,
A weight they carry, a name unsaid.

Their love is duty, cold and thin,
A locked door—I'm trapped within.

But I am more than what they see,
One day, I'll leave—and I'll be free.

18. APRIL 19, 2021

April came like a thief in the night,
Stealing her breath, dimming her light.

I begged, I prayed, I screamed her name,
But all I held was endless pain.

The world moved on, as if it forgot,
But my world stopped in that cruel spot.

A date, a number, etched in stone,
A wound that time has never known.

April is death, April is pain,
A month, a day I curse in vain.

For on that date, the world stayed bright—
But mine was buried in endless night

19. BLANK

20

20. STILL, SHE STAYS

Her mother left,
but did not take her.

She is a body unheld,
a name whispered to no one.

Grief presses into her ribs,
a quiet, endless ache.

She wanted to follow,
to slip into the silence, to let go

but her mother's love
was a promise, not a passing.

So she stays,
not because she wants to,

but because love once given
is never undone.